EVERYONE HAS A LIFE TO LIVE

An American Portrait

BY JERRY GAY

Pulitzer Prize–Winning Photojournalist

**Andrews McMeel
Publishing**

Kansas City

02 03 04 05 06 TWP 10 9 8 7 6 5 4 3 2 1

Library of Congress Cataloging-in-Publication Data
Gay, Jerry.
    Everyone has a life to live : an American portrait / Jerry Gay.
      p.   cm.
    ISBN 0-7407-2496-7
    1. Portrait photography—United States. 2. Gay, Jerry. I. Title.
  TR680.G385 2002
  779'9973—dc21   2001055340

Editors: text—Susan Summers, design—Barbara Witt, production—How It Works

www.theotherjerry.com

BOOK COMPOSITION BY KELLY & COMPANY

For Karyn

Introduction

IN AMERICA we have the ability to see one point of view, or another, or multiple facets of our life at the same time. These photographs represent our country seen from many different angles and timescapes. Yet, they are more. I realized something different was happening when I was taking these photos. The pictures were coming through me but not from me. It was the communion of the moment and the visual gifts shared by the people you see in these photographs. Now, it seemed as if these pictures were developing a life of their own. Later, as I left each person, I felt as if I were leaving a part of me behind but then, too, I knew I was taking something remarkable with me. I had become aware of the forces outside me working with those inside me. As you contemplate the images and see our shared moments and feelings, the pictures become part of you. Great photography speaks to the soul.

Living our lives is much like making a movie. Each day we experience a visual stream of casual information and personal insights. We express ourselves to others and dialogue with our thoughts to create the world around us. We learn that we are responsible for the scenes in our movie, and in the end we understand that really no one was a victim but rather a volunteer. We take control of our film when we examine our lives one frame at a time. Our intentions and thoughts direct the everyday action and eventually create the ending of our movie in this lifetime.

Over the years I have met and photographed holy men, criminals, skid row travelers, heads of state, the famous and not so famous. In the end, I have seen that

we are all the same. Everyone has a story to tell and a life to live. We all share in each other's lives and contribute to the greater movie of life. Just as much as we have each other we have the invisible forces in life that surround each and every one of us. These forces are what bring magic to all areas of our existence. When we observe these hidden voices and intuitive notions we begin to see each other with a new clarity.

The power of each moment is now. This is a book of now moments discovered across America. These moments reflect our past, present, and future choices and speak of our environmental, educational, and social obligations to the generations to come. These images also reflect the overall goodness inside us. The inevitable darkness that surrounds our lives is eclipsed by the inner light we create when we focus on the positive aspects of our movie and believe in this invisible good that surrounds us and guides us at any given moment.

Now, in America, peace is our vision.

Friends are together

even when we are apart.

*Let's not take
ourselves or our friends
too seriously.*

5

We should, however,
take our friendships seriously.

11

*Attempting marriage requires
a good attitude about life.*

13

When we are children,
we learn how to fly . . .

and to believe in our dreams.

When we are children,
we learn we are all the same . . .

and yet we are all different.

25

Work and workers

come in all shapes and sizes.

We are handicapped only when we decide to be.

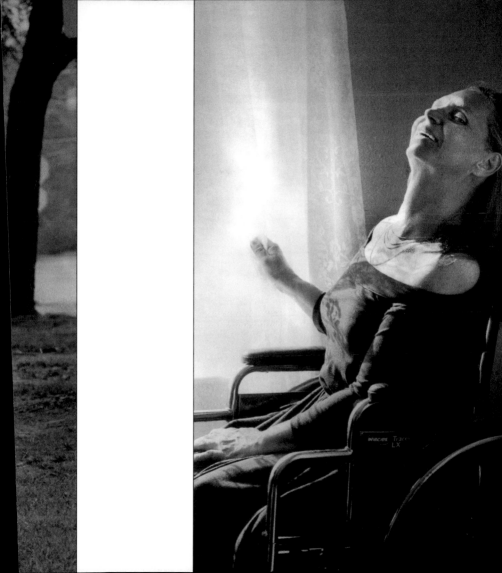

When we hurt others

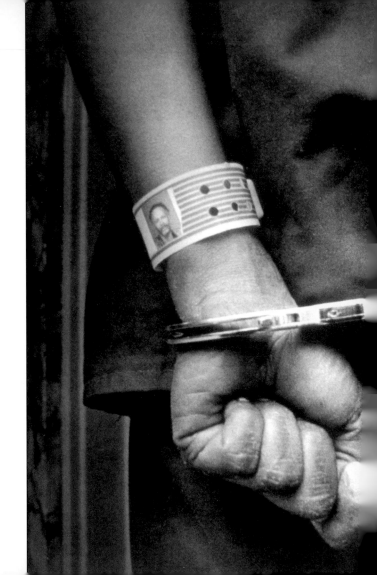

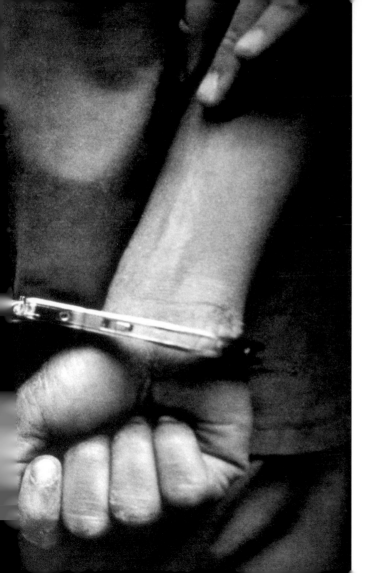

*we do greater harm
to ourselves.*

41

Law and order and punishment

are determined by public opinion.

*When we question
what we believe
we rebuild our
faith in life.*

45

49

We can see
the president's faults

but not our own.

*True freedom
is a state of mind.*

63

When we honor ourselves

Owe honor our country.

DAVID A ...
NORMAN J ...
...WARD L ...
...ALON ...
...HARD D M ...
...UGENE ...
...NA W ...

...ING
...ARDIE
...
...PHILLIP ...
...LIN W ...
...G • CART ...
JAMES D L ...NEST
...E E CRENSBACK JR
LEON L MORRIS
...GLAS L STIGGINS

We must always question
the act of killing another person.

*The quality of life on our planet
is dependent upon the quality of
our thoughts about life.*

79

When we think we really know who we are,
we must have a sense of humor.

In a matter of time,
we become all we
are meant to be.

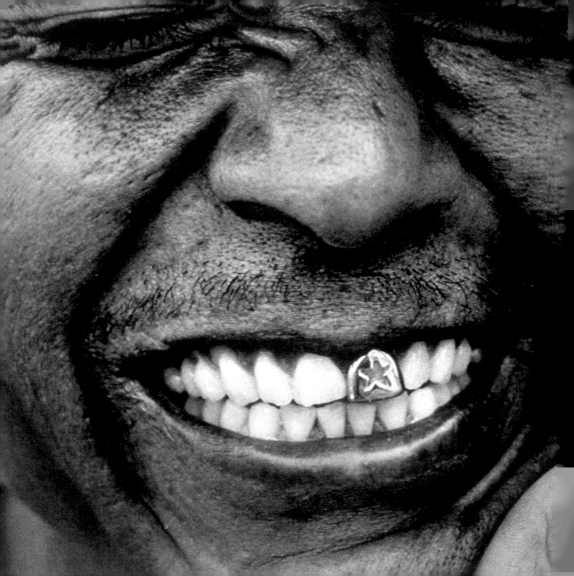

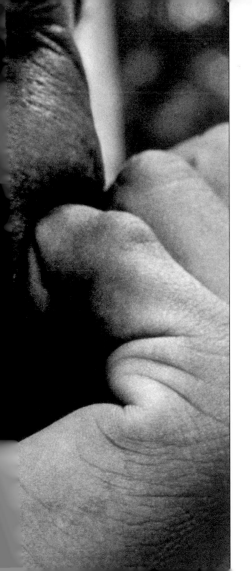

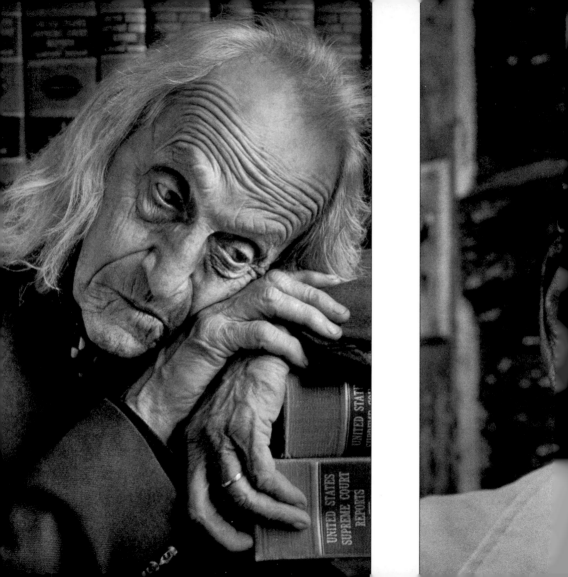

*In a matter of time,
two lives will grow old
together*

*and become one life
shared.*

*Each quiet moment is time
to remember who we are
now, at this moment.*

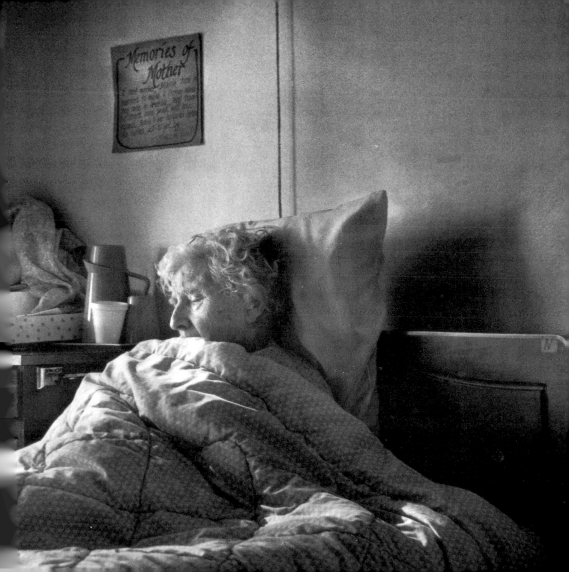

Eternal life is our belief
that life's yet unknown moments
are waiting for us.

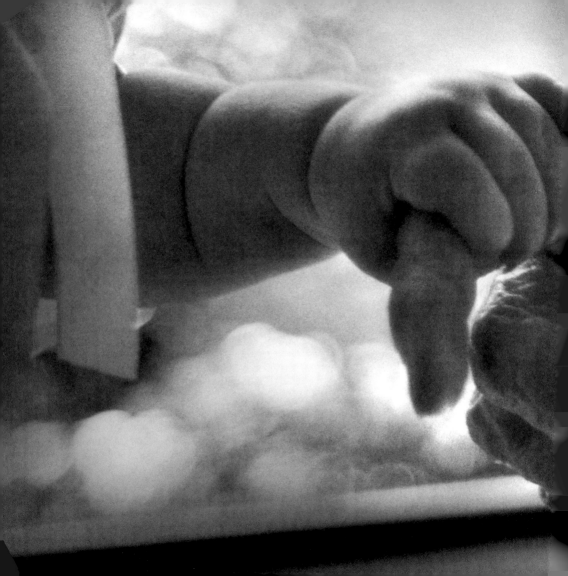

Everyone has a life to live.

Each of us has a story to tell and a life to live.
We all share in each other's lives and contribute
to the greater movie of life.

In the end, we all go to the same dressing room.

The Photojournalist

PHOTOJOURNALIST JERRY GAY is able to recognize and capture on film the heroic among those of us who appear to live ordinary lives in ordinary places. In his own words: "I know I have come to do this in this lifetime."

While a staff photographer for the *Seattle Times,* he was awarded the Pulitzer Prize for news photography in 1975. The prizewinning photograph, *Lull in the Battle,* powerfully depicts firemen in repose after battling a house fire. The photograph speaks of courage, dedication, and humanity during the troubled times of the Vietnam War, when many thought our country was other than courageous, dedicated, or humanitarian.

In addition to the Pulitzer Prize, he received the first Edward Steichen Award for news photography and was named regional Photographer of the Year in 1974, 1975, 1976, and 1977 by the National Press Photographers Association, an organization for which he served as president. Jerry also served on major newspapers across the country, including the *St. Paul Pioneer Press, Los Angeles Times,* and *New York Newsday.*

He lives in La Conner, Washington. Currently, he is a stock photographer for the Stone agency and lectures to schools, media, and corporate organizations regarding responsibilities and possibilities in our ever-changing world.

www.theotherjerry.com